CAJUN COO

DISCOVER CAJUN CUISINE AT ITS FINEST WITH EASY CAJUN RECIPES STRAIGHT FROM THE BAYOU STATE

By
BookSumo Press

Published by
BookSumo
http://www.booksumo.com/

ABOUT THE AUTHOR.

BookSumo Press is a publisher of unique, easy, and healthy cookbooks.

Our cookbooks span all topics and all subjects. If you want a deep dive into the possibilities of cooking with any type of ingredient. Then BookSumo Press is your go to place for robust yet simple and delicious cookbooks and recipes. Whether you are looking for great tasting pressure cooker recipes or authentic ethic and cultural food. BookSumo Press has a delicious and easy cookbook for you.

With simple ingredients, and even simpler step-by-step instructions BookSumo cookbooks get everyone in the kitchen chefing delicious meals.

BookSumo is an independent publisher of books operating in the beautiful Garden State (NJ) and our team of chefs and kitchen experts are here to teach, eat, and be merry!

INTRODUCTION

Welcome to *The Effortless Chef Series*! Thank you for taking the time to purchase this cookbook.

Come take a journey into the delights of easy cooking. The point of this cookbook and all BookSumo Press cookbooks is to exemplify the effortless nature of cooking simply.

In this book we focus on Cajun cooking. You will find that even though the recipes are simple, the taste of the dishes are quite amazing.

So will you take an adventure in simple cooking? If the answer is yes please consult the table of contents to find the dishes you are most interested in.

Once you are ready, jump right in and start cooking.

— BookSumo Press

TABLE OF CONTENTS

Any Issues? Contact Us

If you find that something important to you is missing from this book please contact us at info@booksumo.com.

We will take your concerns into consideration when the 2nd edition of this book is published. And we will keep you updated!

— BookSumo Press

LEGAL NOTES

COMMON ABBREVIATIONS

C.(s)	C.
tbsp	tbsp
tsp	tsp
oz.	oz.
pound	lb

*All units used are standard American measurements

Chapter 1: Easy Cajun Recipes

Cajun Clam Chowder

Ingredients

- 1/4 C. vegetable oil
- 1/4 C. all-purpose flour
- 3-5 tsp Cajun seasoning
- 2 1/2 C. bottled clam juice
- 2 (14 1/2 oz.) cans diced tomatoes, in juice
- 1 (6 oz.) bags baby spinach leaves
- 2 tbsp chopped fresh thyme
- 1 garlic clove, pressed
- 1 lb lump crabmeat

Directions

- Place a large pot over medium heat. Heat the oil in it. Add the flour and mix it well. Let it cook for 2 to 3 min until it becomes golden.
- Mix in it the Cajun seasoning with a pinch of salt. Stir in the clam juice with tomato. Cook them for 4 min.
- Stir in the spinach, thyme, and garlic. Let them cook for an extra 2 min.
- Stir in the crabmeat and cook the stew for an extra 2 minutes. Serve your chowder hot.
- Enjoy.

Servings per Recipe: 6

Timing Information:

Preparation	5 mins
Total Time	12 mins

Nutritional Information:

Calories	192.4
Fat	10.2g
Cholesterol	60.3mg
Sodium	523.1mg
Carbohydrates	6.1g
Protein	18.6g

* Percent Daily Values are based on a 2,000 calorie diet.

Hannah's Macaroni Salad

Ingredients

- 1 (16 oz.) boxes cooked macaroni noodles
- 3 lbs medium unshelled shrimp
- 1 lb of real crabmeat
- 1/4 C. finely chopped red onion
- 1 C. mayonnaise
- 1 C. sour cream
- 1 tbsp spicy mustard
- 1/2 C. butter or 1/2 C. margarine
- 1 tbsp Cajun seasoning
- 1 tbsp Accent seasoning
- 1 tbsp Mrs. Dash seasoning mix
- 1 tsp onion powder
- 1/2 C. sweet relish
- 1/4 tsp cayenne pepper (optional)
- 1 tsp garlic powder

Directions

- Cook the macaroni by following the directions on the package.
- Place a large pan over medium heat. Heat in it the butter. Cook in it the garlic for 1 min.
- Add the shrimp with Cajun seasoning then cook them for 4 min. Turn off the heat and stir in the crabmeat.
- Get a large mixing bowl: Toss in it the macaroni with onion and mayo and sour cream.
- Mix in the Onion powder, Garlic powder, Dash seasning and Sweet Relish. Combine them well.
- Stir the creamy shrimp mix into the salad. Place it in the fridge for at least 2 h then serve it.
- Enjoy.

Servings per Recipe: 20

Timing Information:

Preparation	30 mins
Total Time	40 mins

Nutritional Information:

Calories	225.0
Fat	8.1g
Cholesterol	113.4mg
Sodium	684.1mg
Carbohydrates	20.5g
Protein	16.7g

* Percent Daily Values are based on a 2,000 calorie diet.

Cajun Crawfish Dip

Ingredients

- 2 garlic cloves, grated
- 1/2 C. scallion, thinly sliced, divided
- 1 tbsp butter
- 1 lb crawfish tail
- 1 lb processed cheese, block
- 20 oz. diced tomatoes with green chilies, drained
- 1/2 tsp kosher salt
- 1/4 tsp black pepper, freshly ground, to taste

Directions

- Place a large pot over medium heat. Heat in it the butter. Cook in it the garlic with the white parts of scallions for 2 min.
- Stir in the crawfish and let them cook for 6 min. Transfer the mix to a large mixing bowl.
- Stir the tomato with cheese in the vacant pot. Cook them over medium heat for 2 to 3 min.
- Add to them the crawfish mixture with a pinch of salt and pepper. Cook them for 3 to 4 min. Serve your dip warm.
- Enjoy.

Servings per Recipe: 12

Timing Information:

Preparation	15 mins
Total Time	40 mins

Nutritional Information:

Calories	169.5
Fat	10.7g
Cholesterol	67.2mg
Sodium	925.2mg
Carbohydrates	4.9g
Protein	13.5g

* Percent Daily Values are based on a 2,000 calorie diet.

Cajun Kale Lunch Box

Ingredients

- 2 bunches kale, teared
- 1 (14 oz.) packages extra firm tofu
- 2 tsps Cajun seasoning
- 1 C. carrot, matchsticks
- 2 eggs
- 4 C. water
- 1 tbsp vinegar, for poaching the egg
- 1/4 C. olive oil
- 1 tbsp sesame oil
- 3 tbsp tahini
- 2 tbsp cider vinegar
- 1 inch chunk gingerroot, finely chopped
- 1 tbsp homemade Cajun seasoning
- 1 tbsp sea salt
- 1 tbsp cayenne pepper
- 1 tbsp paprika
- 1 tbsp garlic powder
- 1 tbsp ground black pepper
- 2 tsps onion powder
- 2 tsps oregano
- 2 tsps thyme

Directions

- Before you do anything, preheat the oven to 400 F.
- Place the tofu on a kitchen towel and cover it with another one. Let it rest for 16 min.
- Slice the tofu into long dices and toss them with 2 tsps of Cajun seasoning. Spread them on a lined up baking sheet.
- Cook the tofu dices in the oven for 24 min. Place it aside to cool down.
- Place a large saucepan of water over high heat. Heat it until it starts boiling. Blanch in it the kale for 3 min. Drain it and place it aside.
- Place a saucepan over medium heat. Pour in it 4 C. of water with 1 tbsp of vinegar. Heat it until it starts simmering.
- Crack each egg in a C. Use a wooden spoon to stir the water in around motion in one direction.

- Add to it 1 egg at a time while stirring all the time. Turn the heat off and put on the lid. Let the eggs cook for 4 to 5 min.
- Use a spoon to drain the poached eggs gently.
- Get a mixing bowl: Whisk in it the dressing ingredients and place it aside.
- Place the kale and carrot on 2 serving plates then top each one with tofu. Drizzle over them 1/4 C. of dressing and a poached egg.
- Serve your breakfast plates right away.
- Enjoy.

Servings per Recipe: 2

Timing Information:

Preparation	15 mins
Total Time	35 mins

Nutritional Information:

Calories	749.3
Fat	55.5g
Cholesterol	0.0mg
Sodium	3683.5mg
Carbohydrates	46.9g
Protein	29.7g

* Percent Daily Values are based on a 2,000 calorie diet.

CREOLE SCRAMBLED EGGS

Ingredients

- 1 packages Johnsonville Andouille Fully Cooked Sausage, sliced
- 6 large eggs, beaten
- 1 tsp Cajun seasoning
- 2 tbsp olive oil
- 1 small red skin white potato, diced
- 1 small onion, chopped
- 1/2 medium green pepper, chopped
- 1/2 C. shredded Monterey jack pepper cheese
- 1/2 C. salsa

Directions

- Get a large mixing bowl: Mix in it the eggs with Cajun spice.
- Place a large pan over medium heat. Heat the olive oil in it. Cook in it the potato for 6 min.
- Stir in the onion with pepper and cook them for another 6 min. Stir in the sliced sausage and cook them for 3 min.
- Add the eggs mix and stir them well. Cook them for 3 to 4 minute while stirring it often.
- Stir the cheese into the scramble until it melts. Serve it warm with salsa.
- Enjoy.

Servings per Recipe: 2

Timing Information:

Preparation	10 mins
Total Time	30 mins

Nutritional Information:

Calories	476.6
Fat	36.5g
Cholesterol	583.1mg
Sodium	755.4mg
Carbohydrates	9.9g
Protein	27.3g

* Percent Daily Values are based on a 2,000 calorie diet.

Julia Street Chowder

Ingredients

- 1 tbsp olive oil
- 1/2 lb medium shrimp, peeled, de-veined
- 1/2 C. chopped onion
- 1/2 C. chopped green pepper
- 2 C. frozen Hash Browns, chopped slightly
- 1 cans chicken broth
- 2 tsps Cajun seasoning
- 2 tbsp all-purpose flour
- 2 tbsp water
- 1 cans diced tomatoes, undrained

Directions

- Place a pot over medium heat. Heat the oil in it. Cook in it the shrimp, onion and green pepper for 4 min.
- Stir in the Potatoes, broth and Cajun seasoning. Cook them until they start boiling. Lower the heat and let the soup cook for 24 min.
- Get a small mixing bowl: Combine in it the water with flour. Stir them into the soup followed by the tomato.
- Cook the soup for 6 min then serve it hot.
- Enjoy.

Servings per Recipe: 1

Timing Information:

Preparation	10 mins
Total Time	35 mins

Nutritional Information:

Calories	524.5
Fat	19.4g
Cholesterol	286.4mg
Sodium	2620.9mg
Carbohydrates	42.0g
Protein	46.2g

* Percent Daily Values are based on a 2,000 calorie diet.

ROYAL STREET MEATBALL STEW

Ingredients

- 3/4 C. vegetable oil
- 1 C. all-purpose flour
- 3 C. onions, finely chopped
- 1 1/2 C. bell peppers, finely chopped
- 1 C. celery, finely chopped
- water or beef broth
- 4 garlic cloves, minced
- 2 lbs ground chuck
- 2 large eggs
- 1/4 C. milk
- 1 tbsp Worcestershire sauce
- 1/2 C. fresh parsley, chopped
- 1/3 C. plain breadcrumbs
- salt and cayenne pepper
- 1/4 C. green onion, chopped

Directions

- Place a large pot over medium heat. Heat the oil in it. Mix the flour into it and cook it until it becomes golden brown.
- Mix in it 2 C. of the chopped onion, 1 C. of the bell pepper and 1/2 C. of the celery. Cook them for 5 to 6 min.
- Pour enough broth or water in the pot to fill 2/3 of it. Cook the soup until it starts boiling. Lower the heat and let it cook.
- Get a large mixing bowl: Mix in it the ground chuck, remaining onions, bell pepper, and celery, 2 cloves of the minced garlic and eggs.
- Add the milk with worcestershire sauce, 1/4 C. of the parsley, bread crumbs, and salt and cayenne pepper then mix them well.
- Shape the mix into bite size meatballs. Lower the meatballs into the pot and let them cook for 22 min without stirring them.
- Add the cayenne pepper, rest of the garlic, parsley, green onion and a pinch of salt. Cook the stew for an extra 6 min.
- Serve your stew hot with some rice. Enjoy.

Servings per Recipe: 6

Timing Information:

Preparation	45
Total Time	1 hr 45 mins

Nutritional Information:

Calories	765.9
Fat	55.7g
Cholesterol	167.7mg
Sodium	208.4mg
Carbohydrates	32.3g
Protein	33.3g

* Percent Daily Values are based on a 2,000 calorie diet.

BLACKENED POTATO CRUSTED SHRIMP

Ingredients

- 1 lb jumbo shrimp, shelled and deveined
- 1 tsp blackening seasoning
- 2 C. frozen Hash Browns
- 2 tbsp vegetable oil
- 1 small lemon

Directions

- Get a large mixing bowl: Toss in it the shrimp with Cajun blackening seasoning.
- Place a large pan over medium heat. Heat the oil in it. Press the potato hash into the shrimp then cook them in the hot oil for 4 to 5 min on each side.
- Squeeze over them some fresh lemon juice.
- Enjoy.

Servings per Recipe: 4

Timing Information:

Preparation	15 mins
Total Time	25 mins

Nutritional Information:

Calories	142.8
Fat	7.9g
Cholesterol	143.0mg
Sodium	642.5mg
Carbohydrates	1.7g
Protein	15.5g

* Percent Daily Values are based on a 2,000 calorie diet.

Cajun Vanilla Pie

Ingredients

- 3 medium sweet potatoes, boiled and mashed
- 1/4 C. brown sugar
- 2 tbsp sugar
- 1 tbsp butter
- 1 tbsp pure vanilla extract
- 1 large egg
- 1 tbsp heavy cream
- 1/4 tsp ground cinnamon
- 1 pinch nutmeg
- 1 pinch ground allspice
- 1 9" unbaked pie shell
- 1/2 C. chopped pecans
- 3/4 C. granulated sugar
- 2 large eggs
- 3/4 C. dark corn syrup
- 1 tbsp butter, melted
- 1/2 tsp salt
- ground cinnamon
- 2 tsps pure vanilla extract
- whipped cream

Directions

- Before you do anything, preheat the oven to 300 F.
- Get a large mixing bowl: Beat in it the sweet potatoes, both sugars, butter, vanilla, egg, cinnamon, nutmeg, and allspice until they become smooth.
- Spoon the mix into the pie crust. Garnish it with the pecans.
- Get a mixing bowl: Mix in it the granulated sugar, eggs, corn syrup, melted butter, salt, cinnamon and vanilla.
- Sprinkle the mix over the pecan layer. Place the pie in the oven and let it cook for 1 h 32 min.
- Allow the pie to cool down completely then serve it with your favorite toppings.
- Enjoy.

Servings per Recipe: 8

Timing Information:

| Preparation | 25 mins |
| Total Time | 1 hr 55 mins |

Nutritional Information:

Calories	420.9
Fat	14.7g
Cholesterol	89.5mg
Sodium	337.9mg
Carbohydrates	69.7g
Protein	4.6g

* Percent Daily Values are based on a 2,000 calorie diet.

FRENCH QUARTER GREEN BEANS

Ingredients

- 4 slices thick-sliced bacon, cut into pieces
- 2 small onions, chopped
- 2 garlic cloves
- 3 lbs green beans
- 1/4 C. butter
- 1 pinch of grated nutmeg
- 1/2 C. all-purpose flour
- 1/2 C. heavy cream
- 1 1/2 C. grated white cheddar cheese
- 4 C. chicken broth
- salt and pepper
- 2 (6 oz.) cans fried onions

Directions

- Before you do anything, preheat the oven to 350 F.
- Place a dutch oven over medium heat. Cook in it the bacon for 5 min. Stir into it the onion and cook them for 7 min.
- Stir in the garlic and cook them for 2 min. Place it aside.
- Stir in the green beans with enough broth or water to cover it in a large saucepan.
- Lower the heat put on the lid. Let the mix cook for 30 min. Drain the beans and reserve the cooking liquid.
- Place a large pan over medium heat. Heat in it the butter until it melts. Sauté in it the rest of the onion with salt and nutmeg. Place it aside.
- Cook them for 7 min. Mix in the flour followed by the cream and the reserved bean cooking liquid. Cook it for 6 min until it mixture becomes thick.
- Add the cheese and green beans and cook them for few minutes until the cheese melts.
- Pour the mix into a glass casserole dish. Place it in the oven and let it cook for 26 min. Spread the onion and bacon mix on top.
- Bake it for an extra 14 min. Serve it hot. Enjoy.

Servings per Recipe: 6

Timing Information:

Preparation	30 mins
Total Time	1 hr 30 mins

Nutritional Information:

Calories	438.8
Fat	29.9g
Cholesterol	85.7mg
Sodium	837.1mg
Carbohydrates	27.9g
Protein	18.1g

* Percent Daily Values are based on a 2,000 calorie diet.

HOUMA POTATO POTS

Ingredients

- 1 lb jumbo shrimp, deveined
- 2 large baking potatoes
- 1 C. guacamole
- 3 tbsp Cajun seasoning
- 2 tbsp minced garlic
- 1/2 C. sour cream
- 1 C. shredded cheddar cheese

Directions

- Before you do anything, preheat the grill.
- Place each potato in the middle of piece of foil and wrap it around it. Place it on the grill and let them cook until they become slightly soft.
- Toss the shrimp with Cajun seasoning and garlic in a shallow roasting pan. Place the pan over the grill on the indirect side of it.
- Let the shrimp cook for 12 min. Flip it and let cook for another 12 min.
- Once the shrimp and potato are done place them aside to lose heat for a while.
- Discard the foil sheets and slice them in half. Spoon some of the potato flesh to leave 1/4 of it only.
- Place 4 shrimp aside. Chop the remaining shrimp and place it in the potato shells followed by the cheese.
- Place each one of them in a foil packet. Place them over the grill and let them cook for an extra 12 min.
- Place the 4 shrimps in a small foil packet and grill them for 6 min.
- Once the time is up, top the shrimp layer with guacamole and sour cream. Garnish them with the whole remaining 4 shrimps. Serve them right away.
- Enjoy.

Servings per Recipe: 2

Timing Information:

Preparation	20 mins
Total Time	1 hr 50 mins

Nutritional Information:

Calories	642.4
Fat	32.5g
Cholesterol	375.2mg
Sodium	1689.0mg
Carbohydrates	37.3g
Protein	49.4g

* Percent Daily Values are based on a 2,000 calorie diet.

BAKED SOLE WITH CAULIFLOWER SALAD

Ingredients

- 8 sole fillets
- 3 C. French style green beans
- 3 C. cauliflower, florettes
- 1 tbsp butter
- 1/8 C. lemon juice
- 1 green onion
- salt
- pepper
- cajun seasoning

Directions

- Before you do anything, preheat the oven to 350 F.
- Place the sole fillets on a greased baking pan. Drizzle over them the fresh lemon juice followed by the Cajun seasoning.
- Place the sole sheet in the oven and let it coo for 32 min.
- Place the cauliflower in a heatproof bowl. Cook it in the microwave for 9 min.
- Get a heatproof bowl: Stir in it the green beans with green onion. Cook them in the microwave for 9 min.
- Drain the coked veggies. Add to them the butter with a pinch of salt and pepper. Toss them to coat.
- Serve your baked sole with the veggies salad.
- Enjoy.

Servings per Recipe: 2

Timing Information:

Preparation	10 mins
Total Time	40 mins

Nutritional Information:

Calories	744.6
Fat	14.0g
Cholesterol	328.2mg
Sodium	1111.4mg
Carbohydrates	22.8g
Protein	129.0g

* Percent Daily Values are based on a 2,000 calorie diet.

CREOLE COUNTRY HENS

Ingredients

- 4 oz. hot smoked sausage, chopped
- 1/2 C. long grain white rice
- 1 cans diced tomatoes
- 1/2 C. sliced green onion
- 1/4 C. chopped green bell pepper
- 1 garlic clove, minced
- 1/4 tsp dried thyme leaves
- 4 Cornish hens
- 1 tbsp butter, melted

Directions

- Place a pot over medium heat. Cook in it the sausages for 8 min. Add the rice and let them cook for 3 min.
- Stir in the tomatoes, onions, pepper, garlic and thyme. Cook them until they start boiling. Put on the lid and let them cook for 22 min.
- Spoon the mix into the cavity of the hens. Place them in a greased roasting pan and coat them with butter, a pinch of salt and pepper.
- Place them in the oven and let them cook for 60 min. Allow them to rest for 5 min then serve them warm.
- Enjoy.

Servings per Recipe: 4

Timing Information:

Preparation	10 mins
Total Time	24 hrs 10 mins

Nutritional Information:

Calories	1602.6
Fat	107.1g
Cholesterol	756.2mg
Sodium	389.7mg
Carbohydrates	20.1g
Protein	129.3g

* Percent Daily Values are based on a 2,000 calorie diet.

LAKE CHARLES AVOCADO GLAZED KABOBS

Ingredients

- 20 large uncooked prawns, peeled and deveined
- 2 tbsp Cajun seasoning
- 2 tsps ground cumin
- 1 tsp dried oregano
- 2 garlic cloves, crushed
- 50 ml olive oil
- 1 large avocado
- 2 tbsp sour cream
- 2 tbsp mayonnaise
- 1 tsp Tabasco sauce
- 1/2 tsp garlic powder
- 1 tbsp fresh coriander, chopped
- 1 tbsp lemon juice

Directions

- Get a large mixing bowl: Stir in it the prawns with Cajun seasoning, oregano, cumin, garlic, olive oil, a pinch of salt and pepper.
- Place the mix in the fridge to sit for at least 30 min.
- Before you do anything, preheat the grill and grease it.
- Drain the prawns and thread them into skewers. Place them on the grill and cook them for 4 to 5 min on each side.
- Get a blender: Place in it all the avocado sauce ingredients. Blend them smooth.
- Serve your skewers warm with the avocado sauce.
- Enjoy.

Servings per Recipe: 2

Timing Information:

Preparation	15 mins
Total Time	25 mins

Nutritional Information:

Calories	525.3
Fat	47.7g
Cholesterol	85.6mg
Sodium	482.4mg
Carbohydrates	18.0g
Protein	11.7g

* Percent Daily Values are based on a 2,000 calorie diet.

Cajun Pilaf

Ingredients

- cooking spray
- 1 small brown onion, chopped
- 2 celery ribs, chopped
- 2 garlic cloves, crushed
- 1/4 tsp ground cinnamon
- 2 cloves
- 1/4 tsp ground turmeric
- 3/4 C. long-grain white rice
- 2 C. chicken stock
- 1/4 C. flat leaf parsley, chopped
- 360 g white fish fillets
- 2 tsps Cajun seasoning

Directions

- Place a pot over medium heat. Heat the oil in it. Add the onion, celery and garlic. Let them cook for 6 min.
- Stir in the seasonings and cook them for 1 min. Stir in the rice and cook them for an extra 2 min.
- Pour in the broth and cook them until they start boiling. Lower the heat and put on the lid. Cook the pilaf for 22 min.
- Fold the parsley into te pilaf.
- Place a large pan over medium heat. Heat a splash of oil in it.
- Season the fish fillets with Cajun spice, a pinch of salt and pepper. Cook them in the hot oil for 4 to 6 min on each side.
- Serve your fish fillets warm with the pilaf.
- Enjoy.

Servings per Recipe: 2

Timing Information:

Preparation	10 mins
Total Time	30 mins

Nutritional Information:

Calories	530.8
Fat	5.9g
Cholesterol	127.8mg
Sodium	514.2mg
Carbohydrates	70.5g
Protein	45.0g

* Percent Daily Values are based on a 2,000 calorie diet.

CAJUN TORTILLAS PAN

Ingredients

- 2 tbsp butter
- 1/2 C. green bell pepper, chopped
- 1/2 C. onion, chopped
- 2 jalapeno peppers, chopped
- 4 oz. green chilies, chopped
- 10 oz. condensed cream of chicken soup
- 10 oz. Rotel tomatoes & chilies
- 2 C. cooked chicken, cubes
- 6 flour tortillas, chopped
- 1 1/2 C. shredded cheddar cheese
- sour cream
- green onion
- sliced avocado

Directions

- Before you do anything, preheat the oven to 325 F.
- Place a pot over medium heat. Heat in it the butter. Sauté in it the onion with pepper and jalapenos for 6 min.
- Stir in the green chiles, soup, Rotel tomatoes, and chicken.
- Lay 1/3 of the tortillas in a greased baking dish. Spread over it 1/3 of the chicken mix followed by 1/3 of the cheese.
- Repeat the process to make an extra 2 layers. Place the pan in the oven and let it cook for 35 min. Serve it hot.
- Enjoy.

Servings per Recipe: 4

Timing Information:

Preparation	20 mins
Total Time	50 mins

Nutritional Information:

Calories	407.5
Fat	18.1g
Cholesterol	73.4mg
Sodium	1131.2mg
Carbohydrates	36.7g
Protein	24.4g

* Percent Daily Values are based on a 2,000 calorie diet.

CREOLE SUMMER WATERMELON RELISH

Ingredients

- 5 C. watermelon rind, diced
- 1 large onion, diced
- 1 red bell pepper, diced
- 1 green bell pepper, diced
- 1-2 fresh jalapeno pepper, sliced
- 1 C. sugar
- 2 C. vinegar
- 1 tbsp pickling salt
- 1/2 tsp mustard, seed
- 1 bay leaf
- 1 tsp celery seed
- 1 tsp peppercorns
- 1 tsp pepper, flakes

Directions

- Get a large mixing bowl: Stir in it the onion with rind, peppers, and salt. Pour over them enough cold water to cover them.
- Place the bowl in the fridge and let it sit for an overnight.
- Get a large pot. Stir in it the sugar with vinegar, mustard, bay leaf, celery seed, peppercorns, and pepper flakes.
- Cook them over medium heat until they start boiling. Drain the rind and onion mix then stir it into the pot.
- Cook them until they start boiling again. Lower the heat and bring to a simmer.
- Spoon the mix into sterilized jars leaving 1/2 of space empty in each jar. Seal the jars and place them in a some hot water for 12 min.
- Let them sit for at least 1 week before serving it.
- Enjoy.

Servings per Recipe: 40

Timing Information:

Preparation	30 mins
Total Time	55 mins

Nutritional Information:

Calories	25.0
Fat	0.0g
Cholesterol	0.0mg
Sodium	175.8mg
Carbohydrates	5.7g
Protein	0.1g

* Percent Daily Values are based on a 2,000 calorie diet.

CREOLE STUFFED PEPPERS

Ingredients

- 6-10 large bell peppers, tops and insides removed
- 4 C. cooked rice
- 24-32 oz. tomato sauce
- 1 cans diced tomatoes & chilies
- 1 large onion, chopped
- 1 medium bell pepper, chopped
- 1-2 tbsp minced garlic
- Cajun seasoning
- 1 lb ground beef
- 1 lb ground sausage

Directions

- Before you do anything, preheat the oven to 350 F.
- Place a large pan over medium heat. Cook in it the ground beef and ground sausage for 10 min. Discard the excess grease.
- Stir in the seasonings, veggies, diced tomatoes, and tomato sauce. Cook them until the veggies are soft. Drain 2 C. of sauce from the mix and place it aside.
- Stir in the rice into the pan and turn off the heat to make the filling. Spoon the mix into the bell peppers.
- Place them in a greased casserole dish. Pour the reserve sauce all over it. Cook it in the oven for 60 min.
- Serve your stuffed peppers warm.
- Enjoy.

Servings per Recipe: 6

Timing Information:

Preparation	45 mins
Total Time	1 hr 45 mins

Nutritional Information:

Calories	636.9
Fat	32.2g
Cholesterol	105.8mg
Sodium	1325.7mg
Carbohydrates	54.6g
Protein	32.1g

* Percent Daily Values are based on a 2,000 calorie diet.

CAJUN TEX GUMBO

Ingredients

- 1/4 C. all-purpose flour
- 1 tsp salt
- 1/2 tsp black pepper
- 1/4 tsp cayenne
- 1 tsp paprika
- 1/2 tsp onion powder
- 1/2 tsp garlic powder
- 6 chicken breasts, cubed
- 1/4 C. vegetable oil
- 1 C. all-purpose flour
- 1 C. lard
- 2 C. chopped onions
- 1 1/2 C. chopped green bell peppers
- 1 1/2 C. chopped celery
- 2 quarts chicken stock
- 3/4 lb andouille sausage, cubed
- 2 garlic cloves, minced
- 3 C. cooked rice

Directions

- Get a large mixing bowl: Toss in it the spices with chicken and 1/4 C. of flour.
- Place a large pan over medium heat. Heat the oil in it. Add the chicken in batches and coo them for 5 min per batch.
- Place a pot over medium heat. Melt the lard in it. Add the flour and mix it well then cook it until it becomes golden brown.
- Add the veggies and mix them well. Add to it the stock gradually while mixing them all the time.
- Cook them until they start boiling. Stir in the chicken, sausage, and garlic. Lower the heat and let the stew cook for 60 min.
- Adjust the seasoning of your gumbo then serve it warm.
- Enjoy.

Servings per Recipe: 6

Timing Information:

Preparation	40 mins
Total Time	1 hr 25 mins

Nutritional Information:

Calories	1201.9
Fat	76.6g
Cholesterol	167.2mg
Sodium	1645.3mg
Carbohydrates	69.0g
Protein	55.2g

* Percent Daily Values are based on a 2,000 calorie diet.

QUICK CAJUN GUMBO

Ingredients

- 1 box Zatarians gumbo base mix
- 1 lb chicken
- 1 lb smoked sausage
- 1 boxes sliced frozen okra, defrosted
- 2 C. long grain white rice
- 1/2 tbsp salt

Directions

- Cook the rice by following the instructions on the package.
- Prepare the gumbo mix by following the instructions on the package.
- Pour the mix into a large pot over high heat. Cook it until it starts boiling while stirring it all the time.
- Stir in the meat and cook them until they start boiling again. Lower the heat and let the stew coo for 30 min while stirring it from time to time.
- Add the okra and cook them until they start boiling again. Serve your gumbo with white rice.
- Enjoy.

Servings per Recipe: 8

Timing Information:

Preparation	1 hr
Total Time	1 hr 35 mins

Nutritional Information:

Calories	475.9
Fat	24.9g
Cholesterol	77.2mg
Sodium	963.7mg
Carbohydrates	39.4g
Protein	21.2g

* Percent Daily Values are based on a 2,000 calorie diet.

CREOLE CRAB CAKES

Ingredients

- 2 roasted red peppers
- 1/2 C. fat-free mayonnaise
- 1/4-1/2 tsp cayenne pepper
- 1/2 tsp seasoning salt
- 3 tsps olive oil, divided
- 1/2 onion, chopped
- 1 stalk celery, chopped
- 2 eggs, beaten
- 2 tbsp ground walnuts
- 2 tbsp chopped fresh parsley
- 2 tbsp fat-free mayonnaise
- 1 tbsp lemon juice
- 1 tsp Cajun seasoning
- 1/2 tsp crab boil seasoning
- 2 tsps Worcestershire sauce
- 1/2 tsp mustard powder
- 1/4 tsp crushed celery seed
- 1/2 tsp ground paprika
- 1 lb crawfish meat or 1 lb crabmeat
- 1/2-1 tsp hot pepper sauce
- 1 C. whole wheat breadcrumbs

Directions

- Get a food processor: Place in it the roasted peppers then process them until they become smooth.
- Pour in the mayonnaise and spices then blend them smooth to make the sauce. Place it in the fridge.
- Get a large mixing bowl: Combine in it all the ingredients except for the bread crumbs. Shape the mix into 8 cakes then roll them in the breadcrumbs.
- Place a large pan over medium heat. Heat 2 tsps of olive oil. Cook in it the fish cakes for 3 to 4 min on each side.
- Serve your fish cakes warm with the pepper sauce.
- Enjoy.

Servings per Recipe: 8

Timing Information:

Preparation	30 mins
Total Time	40 mins

Nutritional Information:

Calories	173.2
Fat	6.1g
Cholesterol	115.6mg
Sodium	378.7mg
Carbohydrates	17.3g
Protein	13.2g

* Percent Daily Values are based on a 2,000 calorie diet.

Baton Rouge Cabbage Stew

Ingredients

- 26 oz. pasta sauce
- 26 oz. extra mild salsa
- 1 lb ground meat
- 2 large heads of cabbage
- salt and pepper
- 8 oz. water or 8 oz. chicken stock

Directions

- Bring a large salted pot of water to a boil. Core the cabbage and slice it into 1/2 inch thick slices.
- Cook them in the hot water for 3 to 4 min until they wilt.
- Place a pot over medium heat. Cook in it the meat for 8 min. Disard the excess grease. Rinse the cooked meat and drain it.
- Stir the cooked meat back in the pot with sauce, and salsa to wilted cabbage. Let it cook for 8 min.
- Serve your un-rolled cabbage stew warm.
- Enjoy.

Servings per Recipe: 12

Timing Information:

Preparation	20 mins
Total Time	35 mins

Nutritional Information:

Calories	111.9
Fat	1.8g
Cholesterol	0.0mg
Sodium	701.8mg
Carbohydrates	22.3g
Protein	5.1g

* Percent Daily Values are based on a 2,000 calorie diet.

Spicy Mayo Salad

Ingredients

- 3 cans corn, drained
- 2 C. shredded cheddar cheese
- 1 small purple onion, diced
- 1 medium bell pepper, sliced
- 1 C. Hellmann's mayonnaise
- 1 (11 1/2 oz.) bag Fritos corn chips
- lots cracked black pepper

Directions

- Get a large mixing bowl: Stir in it the corn with cheese, onion, pepper, and mayonnaise.
- Place the salad in the fridge for few hours.
- Top the salad with the Fritos chips.
- Enjoy.

Servings per Recipe: 8

Timing Information:

Preparation	10 mins
Total Time	10 mins

Nutritional Information:

Calories	404.0
Fat	22.3g
Cholesterol	7.6mg
Sodium	746.6mg
Carbohydrates	50.7g
Protein	5.2g

* Percent Daily Values are based on a 2,000 calorie diet.

CREOLE SPRING ROLLS

Ingredients

- 1/2 lb andouille sausage, diced
- 6 cloves garlic, minced
- 1 medium onion, minced
- 1 cans black beans
- 1 avocado, diced
- 1/4 lb cheddar cheese, grated
- 2 tbsp fresh cilantro, chopped
- 1 ear corn, roasted
- 1 roasted red bell pepper
- 1 pinch cumin
- 1 pinch chili powder
- salt and pepper
- 15-20 eggroll wraps
- oil

Directions

- Place a large pan over medium heat. Cook in it the sausage for 5 min. Add the onion with garlic and cook them for 10 min to make the filling.
- Turn off the heat and spoon the mix into a mixing bowl to cool down.
- Lay a wrapper on a working surface with the pointed corner facing towards you. Brush its edges with some water.
- Place 3 tbsp of the filling in the middle of the wrapper then pull the pointed corner on top of it and press it to seal it.
- brush the right and left corner over the filling and press them to seal them.
- Repeat the process with the remaining ingredients.
- Place a large pan over medium heat. Heat in it 1 inch of oil. Cook in it the rolls in the batches until they become golden brown.
- Serve your crunchy rolls with your favorite sauce. Enjoy.

Servings per Recipe: 10

Timing Information:

Preparation	30 mins
Total Time	40 mins

Nutritional Information:

Calories	361.5
Fat	14.1g
Cholesterol	29.1mg
Sodium	630.0mg
Carbohydrates	43.6g
Protein	15.8g

* Percent Daily Values are based on a 2,000 calorie diet.

SHREVEPORT STEW

Ingredients

- 1 tsp olive oil
- 1 lb hot Italian sausage
- 1 lb white fish fillet, chunks
- 1 lb sea scallops
- 1 lb shrimp
- 2 red bell peppers, chopped
- 2 stalks celery, chopped
- 1 large onion, chopped
- 1 tbsp basil leaves, crushed
- 1 tbsp oregano leaves, crushed
- 2-3 cloves garlic, crushed
- 4 cans diced tomatoes

Directions

- Place a Dutch oven over medium heat. Cook in it the sausage for 8 min.
- Stir in the Basil, oregano and Garlic, onion, celery& pepper. Cook them for 22 min.
- Stir in the tomato and let them cook for an extra 22 min. Fold the seafood into the mix and let them cook for 6 to 8 min until they are done.
- Serve your stew hot with some pasta.
- Enjoy.

Servings per Recipe: 8

Timing Information:

Preparation	20 mins
Total Time	1 hr 20 mins

Nutritional Information:

Calories	431.4
Fat	18.3g
Cholesterol	199.6mg
Sodium	1415.0mg
Carbohydrates	21.5g
Protein	44.9g

* Percent Daily Values are based on a 2,000 calorie diet.

Southern Lunch Box

(Spicy Corn Salad)

Ingredients

- 17 1/2 oz. cook frozen kernel corn
- 1 green bell pepper, diced
- 1 red bell pepper, diced
- 1 C. hot pickled okra or 6 green onions
- 1/2 C. parsley, minced
- 1 C. cherry tomatoes, halved
- 1 tsp sugar
- 1/4 C. wine vinegar
- 1 tsp creole mustard
- 1 tbsp dried basil leaves
- 2 tbsp mayonnaise
- 1/2 tsp black pepper
- 1/2 tsp Tabasco sauce
- salt
- 1/2 C. olive oil

Tabasco:

Directions

- Get a large mixing bowl: Stir in it all the salad ingredients.
- Get a small mixing bowl: Whisk in it the sauce ingredients except of the oil.
- Add to it the olive oil in a steady stream while whisking it all the time. Drizzle the sauce over the salad.
- Place it in the fridge for an overnight then serve it.
- Enjoy.

Servings per Recipe: 6

Timing Information:

Preparation	0 mins
Total Time	8 hrs

Nutritional Information:

Calories	269.9
Fat	20.7g
Cholesterol	1.2mg
Sodium	331.2mg
Carbohydrates	21.8g
Protein	3.2g

* Percent Daily Values are based on a 2,000 calorie diet.

CREOLE SEAFOOD FILLETS

Ingredients

- 4 fish fillets
- butter-flavored cooking spray
- 2 tsps Cajun seasoning
- 1/4 C. seasoned breadcrumbs
- salt and pepper

Directions

- Before you do anything, preheat the oven to 400 F.
- Place the fish fillets on a lined up baking sheet. Grease them with a cooking spray.
- Season them with the Cajun spice then top them with the bread crumbs.
- Place the fish pan in the oven. Cook it in the oven for 4 to 6 min. Serve it warm.
- Enjoy.

Servings per Recipe: 2

Timing Information:

Preparation	5 mins
Total Time	15 mins

Nutritional Information:

Calories	435.4
Fat	3.9g
Cholesterol	198.1mg
Sodium	544.6mg
Carbohydrates	10.2g
Protein	84.3g

* Percent Daily Values are based on a 2,000 calorie diet.

CREOLE ALFREDO

Ingredients

- 1 1/2-2 lbs boneless skinless chicken
- garlic soup mix
- 8 oz. cream cheese
- 1 cans cream of chicken soup
- 1 cans cream of mushroom soup
- 1 cans water
- 2 chicken bouillon cubes
- 1-2 tbsp Cajun seasoning
- 1/4 tsp lemon pepper
- canned mushroom
- 8 oz. parmesan cheese
- linguine

Directions

- Stir the chicken with soup mix, cream cheese, mushroom soup, water, bouillon cubes, Cajun seasoning, lemon pepper, some canned mushroom, a pinch of salt and pepper.
- In a greased slow cooker. Put on the lid and let them cook for 4 h on low.
- Stir in the cheese until it melts. Serve your alfredo sauce with some pasta.
- Enjoy.

Servings per Recipe: 4

Timing Information:

Preparation	5 mins
Total Time	4 hrs 5 mins

Nutritional Information:

Calories	763.0
Fat	48.6g
Cholesterol	227.6mg
Sodium	2723.5mg
Carbohydrates	14.8g
Protein	64.6g

* Percent Daily Values are based on a 2,000 calorie diet.

CREOLE RUMP ROLLS

Ingredients

- 500 g beef rump, sliced
- 1 yellow onion, sliced
- 1 red capsicum, sliced
- 2 tbsp Cajun seasoning
- 3 medium tomatoes, wedges
- 1 French baguette
- lettuce leaf

Directions

- Place a large pan over medium heat. Heat the oil in it. Cook in it the beef for 8 min. Drain it and place it aside.
- Sauté in it the onion with capsicum and seasoning for 5 min in the same pan.
- Stir in the tomato wedges and cook them for 16 min over low heat. Add the browned beef to the pan.
- Slice the baguette open and lay in it the lettuce leaves. Spoon over it the beef mix. Serve it with your favorite toppings.
- Enjoy.

Servings per Recipe: 4

Timing Information:

Preparation	10 mins
Total Time	35 mins

Nutritional Information:

Calories	566.6
Fat	15.4g
Cholesterol	76.2mg
Sodium	759.1mg
Carbohydrates	67.0g
Protein	38.1g

* Percent Daily Values are based on a 2,000 calorie diet.

LEMON CREOLE CHICKEN

Ingredients

- 1/2 C. lemon juice
- 1/4 C. hot pepper sauce
- 3 tbsp Cajun seasoning
- 2 lbs chicken

Directions

- Before you do anything, preheat the oven to 350 F.
- Stir all the ingredients in a greased baking dish.
- Place it in the oven and let it cook for 48 min. Serve your chicken casserole warm.
- Enjoy.

Servings per Recipe: 6

Timing Information:

Preparation	10 mins
Total Time	50 mins

Nutritional Information:

Calories	203.9
Fat	13.8g
Cholesterol	69.0mg
Sodium	313.0mg
Carbohydrates	1.9g
Protein	17.2g

* Percent Daily Values are based on a 2,000 calorie diet.

HOMEMADE SPICY MUSTARD

Ingredients

- 2 oz. dry mustard
- 1 tbsp flour
- 3 tbsp malt vinegar
- 1 tbsp honey
- 1 clove garlic, chopped
- 1 tbsp hot pepper flakes
- 1 tsp cumin
- 1 tsp thyme
- 1 tsp black pepper
- 1 tsp paprika

Directions

- Get a mixing bowl: Stir in it the flour with mustard. Add to it 1/4 C. of cold water while mixing them all the time.
- Let the mustard sauce sit for 16 min. Add the rest of the ingredients and mix them well. Serve your sauce whenever you desire.
- Enjoy.

Servings per Recipe: 1

Timing Information:

Preparation	15 mins
Total Time	15 mins

Nutritional Information:

Calories	851.0
Fat	43.4g
Cholesterol	0.0mg
Sodium	38.9mg
Carbohydrates	93.4g
Protein	34.3g

* Percent Daily Values are based on a 2,000 calorie diet.

CREOLE PIZZA

Ingredients

- 1 large pizza crusts
- 1/2 lb sausage, cooked, crumbled
- 2 chicken breasts, cooked, strips
- 1 small zucchini, sliced
- 1 red bell pepper, diced
- 1/2 C. chopped onion
- 2 cloves chopped garlic
- 1 cans tomato sauce
- 1 cans diced tomatoes
- 1 tbsp brown mustard
- 1 tbsp chopped fresh ginger
- 2 tsps brown sugar
- 2 tsps Worcestershire sauce
- 2 tsps cumin
- 2 tsps other Cajun seasoning
- 1/2 tsp oregano
- 1 dash hot sauce, to taste
- 8 oz. grated cheese

Directions

- Before you do anything, preheat the oven to 350 F.
- Get a food processor: Combine in it the onions, tomato sauce, tomatoes, brown sugar, garlic, ginger, and all the seasonings.
- Pulse them several times until they become puréed to make the sauce.
- Transfer the sauce to a heavy saucepan. Let it cook for 35 min.
- Place the pizza crust on a lined up baking sheet. Top it wit half of the sauce followed by the zucchini slices and chicken.
- Top them with the sausage and bell peppers. Drizzle the remaining sauce on top with cheese.
- Place the pizza in the oven and let it cook for 16 min. Serve it hot.
- Enjoy.

Servings per Recipe: 4

Timing Information:

Preparation	30 mins
Total Time	1 hr

Nutritional Information:

Calories	611.9
Fat	37.6g
Cholesterol	115.5mg
Sodium	1530.6mg
Carbohydrates	33.1g
Protein	37.2g

* Percent Daily Values are based on a 2,000 calorie diet.

CREOLE SHRIMP TORTILLAS

Ingredients

- 1/2 C. uncooked rice
- 1 tbsp olive oil
- 1 lb uncooked medium shrimp, peeled and deveined
- 1 small red onion, chopped
- 1 tbsp minced garlic
- 2 tsps Cajun seasoning
- 1 C. tomato sauce
- 8 8-inch flour tortillas, warmed

Directions

- Cook the rice by following the instructions on the package.
- Place a large pan over medium heat. Heat the oil in it. Cook in it the shrimp, onion, garlic, and Cajun seasoning for 4 min.
- Mix in it the pasta sauce with cooked rice. Divide the mix between the tortillas and wrap them. Serve them right away.
- Enjoy.

Servings per Recipe: 8

Timing Information:

Preparation	30 mins
Total Time	40 mins

Nutritional Information:

Calories	306.6
Fat	6.9g
Cholesterol	86.4mg
Sodium	469.2mg
Carbohydrates	42.1g
Protein	17.3g

* Percent Daily Values are based on a 2,000 calorie diet.

CREOLE ICE CREAM

Ingredients

- 2 1/2 C. heavy cream
- 1 C. whole milk
- 3/4 C. dark brown sugar
- 5 egg yolks
- 1 C. sweet potato puree, canned
- 1/4 tsp ground nutmeg
- 3/4 tsp ground cinnamon
- 1/2 tsp cayenne pepper
- 1 1/2 tbsp dried rosemary
- 1/4 C. pecans, lightly chopped

Directions

- Place a heavy saucepan over medium heat. Stir in it the cream, milk, and brown sugar until they become hot.
- Get a mixing bowl: Beat in it the eggs while adding 1 C. hot cream mix gradually. Stir the mix into the saucepan gradually while mixing all the time.
- Let it cook over medium heat while stirring all the time until it becomes slightly thick for 7 min.
- Once the again, pour the mix into a large mixing bowl. Add to it the sweet potato puree, nutmeg, cinnamon, cayenne pepper and rosemary. Mix them well.
- Cover the bowl with a plastic wrap and place it in the fridge for 2 h 30 min.
- Once the time is up, prepare the ice cream by following the manufacturer's instructions. Serve it with your favorite toppings.
- Enjoy.

Servings per Recipe: 1

Timing Information:

Preparation	3 hrs
Total Time	6 hrs

Nutritional Information:

Calories	3547.7
Fat	269.6g
Cholesterol	1669.5mg
Sodium	608.2mg
Carbohydrates	261.3g
Protein	40.2g

* Percent Daily Values are based on a 2,000 calorie diet.

Cajun Sausage Kabobs

Ingredients

- 1 andouille sausages, sliced
- 1 green bell pepper, chopped
- 1 red bell pepper, chopped
- 1 yellow bell pepper, chopped
- 1 onion, diced
- 1 tbsp Cajun seasoning
- skewer

Directions

- Before you do anything, preheat the grill and grease it.
- Thread the sausage slices with bell peppers and onion into the skewers while alternating between them.
- Season them with the Cajun seasoning, a pinch of salt and pepper. Cook the kabobs on the grill for 16 min or until they are done.
- Serve your kabobs with your favorite sauce.
- Enjoy.

Servings per Recipe: 4

Timing Information:

Preparation	10 mins
Total Time	25 mins

Nutritional Information:

Calories	333.5
Fat	23.6g
Cholesterol	48.8mg
Sodium	1038.6mg
Carbohydrates	12.3g
Protein	17.7g

* Percent Daily Values are based on a 2,000 calorie diet.

CREOLE SHRIMP BITES

Ingredients

- 2 tbsp parsley, minced
- 2 tbsp green onions, minced
- 2 tbsp butter
- 2 tbsp flour
- 1/2 C. milk
- 1/2 tsp salt
- 1/4 tsp hot pepper sauce
- 1/2 lb shrimp, cooked
- 2 eggs
- 2 C. breadcrumbs
- oil, for frying

Directions

- Place a saucepan over medium heat. Heat in it the butter. Add the green onions with parsley and cook them for 1 min.
- Add the flour and mix them well. Pour in the milk with hot sauce and a pinch of salt. Whisk them until they become smooth.
- Let them cook until they become thick. Turn off the heat and fold the shrimp into the mix.
- Allow the mix to cool down for a while then shape it into bite size balls.
- Whisk the eggs in a shallow bowl. Lower in it the shrimp balls then coat them with the bread crumbs, dip them again in the eggs and roll them in the breadcrumbs.
- Place them on a lined up baking sheet. Place the shrimp balls in the fridge and let them sit for 32 min.
- Place a large skillet over medium heat. Heat 1/4 to 1/2 inch of oil in it. Add the shrimp balls and cook them for 4 min until they become golden brown.
- Drain the shrimp balls then serve them with your favorite dip.
- Enjoy.

Servings per Recipe: 1

Timing Information:

Preparation	45 mins
Total Time	1 hr 5 mins

Nutritional Information:

Calories	62.6
Fat	2.1g
Cholesterol	30.6mg
Sodium	186.2mg
Carbohydrates	7.3g
Protein	3.2g

* Percent Daily Values are based on a 2,000 calorie diet.

CREOLE FRIED CRABS

Ingredients

- 3 tsps canola oil, divided
- 1 small onion, finely diced
- 1/2 C. finely diced green bell pepper
- 1/2 C. frozen corn kernels, thawed
- 1 1/2 tsps Cajun seasoning, divided
- 1 lb pasteurized crabmeat
- 1 large egg white

- 3/4 C. plain breadcrumbs
- 1/4 C. mayonnaise
- 1/2 tsp grated lemon zest
- 1/4 C. mayonnaise
- 2 tbsp sour cream
- 2 scallions, chopped
- 2 tsps capers
- 1 tbsp Dijon mustard
- 1 tbsp sweet relish
- 1/4 tsp ground pepper

Directions

- Before you do anything, preheat the oven to 425 F.
- Place a large pan over medium heat. Heat in it 1 tsp of oil. Sauté in it the onion, bell pepper, corn and 1 tsp Cajun seasoning for 5 miin.
- Drain them and transfer them to a mixing bowl. Let it sit for 6 min. Mix in the crab, egg white, 1/2 C. breadcrumbs, mayonnaise and lemon zest.
- Shape the mix into 8 cakes and place them on a lined up baking pan.
- Get a small mixing bowl: Stir in it 1/4 C. breadcrumbs, 1/2 tsp Cajun seasoning and 2 tsps oil. Press the mix into the crab cakes.
- Cook them in the oven for 22 min.
- To make the sauce: mayonnaise, sour cream, scallions, capers, mustard, relish and pepper. Serve it with the crab cakes.
- Get a mixing bowl: Whisk in it the
- Enjoy.

Servings per Recipe: 4

Timing Information:

Preparation	15 mins
Total Time	45 mins

Nutritional Information:

Calories	360.5
Fat	16.2g
Cholesterol	61.0mg
Sodium	1469.2mg
Carbohydrates	27.0g
Protein	26.0g

* Percent Daily Values are based on a 2,000 calorie diet.

SPICY GINGER CAKE

Ingredients

- 2 eggs
- 3/4 C. dark brown sugar, packed
- 3/4 C. light molasses
- 3/4 C. butter, melted
- 2 1/2 C. all-purpose flour
- 2 tsps ground ginger
- 1 1/2 tsps ground cinnamon
- 1/2 tsp ground cloves
- 1/2 tsp ground nutmeg
- 1/2 tsp baking soda
- 1/2 tsp salt
- 1 C. boiling water
- 1 C. pecans, chopped

Directions

- Before you do anything, preheat the oven to 350 F.
- Get a large mixing bowl: Mix in it the eggs, brown sugar, molasses and melted butter.
- Add to it the rest of the ingredients and combine them well. Add the boiling water and mix them well.
- Transfer the mix to a greased cake pan. Cook it in the oven for 36 min.
- Allow the cake to cool down completely then serve it.
- Enjoy.

Servings per Recipe: 12

Timing Information:

Preparation	10 mins
Total Time	45 mins

Nutritional Information:

Calories	387.0
Fat	19.2g
Cholesterol	65.7mg
Sodium	257.2mg
Carbohydrates	50.8g
Protein	4.7g

* Percent Daily Values are based on a 2,000 calorie diet.

Herbed Chicken and Cajun Skillet

Ingredients

- 3/4 lb skinless chicken breast, cubes
- 1/2 lb turkey kielbasa, slices
- 1 medium onion, chopped
- 3 garlic cloves, minced
- 1 tbsp olive oil
- 1 medium green pepper, chopped
- 1 medium sweet red pepper, chopped
- 1 medium yellow pepper, chopped
- 1 lb fresh mushrooms, sliced
- 2 medium tomatoes, diced
- minced fresh herbs
- 1 1/2 tsps Cajun seasoning
- 1/2 tsp salt
- 1/4 tsp pepper
- 1 tbsp cornstarch
- 2 tbsp cold water
- cooked spaghetti

Directions

- Place a large pan over medium heat. Heat the oil in it. Cook in it the chicken, kielbasa, onion and garlic for 5 min.
- Stir in it the peppers, mushrooms, tomatoes, herbs, Cajun seasoning, salt and pepper. Let them cook for 8 min.
- Get a small mixing bowl: Whisk in it the cornstarch with water. Stir them into the pan. Cook them until they start boiling.
- Let them cook for 3 min. Serve your stir fry warm.
- Enjoy.

Servings per Recipe: 8

Timing Information:

Preparation	20 mins
Total Time	20 mins

Nutritional Information:

Calories	104.3
Fat	2.6g
Cholesterol	24.6mg
Sodium	179.4mg
Carbohydrates	8.8g
Protein	12.5g

* Percent Daily Values are based on a 2,000 calorie diet.

MILD CAJUN EGGPLANT CASSEROLE

Ingredients

- 1 1/2 C. all-purpose flour
- 3 large eggs
- 1 C. milk
- 4 C. breadcrumbs
- 1 1/2 large eggplants, sliced
- 8 tbsp olive oil
- 2 1/2 C. mild salsa
- 1/2 lb tasso or 1/2 lb hot capocollo, chopped
- 1/2 lb andouille sausages or 1/2 lb beef links, chopped
- 2 C. cheddar cheese, grated
- 2 C. cheddar cheese, grated

Directions

- Before you do anything, preheat the oven to 350 F.
- Get a large mixing bowl: Mix in it eggs with milk.
- Dust an eggplant slice with flour then coat it with milk mix and roll it in the breadcrumbs. Place it on a lined up bakin pan.
- Repeat the process with the remaining ingredients.
- Place a large pan over medium heat. Heat in it 2 tbsp of oil. Fry in it the eggplant slices for 4 min on each side.
- Lay half of the eggplant slices in a greased baking dish. Top it with 1 1/2 of salsa, all the ham and sausage. Sprinkle 1 1/2 C. of cheese over it.
- Lay the remaining eggplant slices on top then spread the remaining salsa over it followed by the remaining cheese.
- Place the pan in the oven and let it cook for 46 min. Serve it hot.
- Enjoy.

Servings per Recipe: 6

Timing Information:

Preparation	30 mins
Total Time	2 hrs

Nutritional Information:

Calories	936.7
Fat	61.1g
Cholesterol	218.7mg
Sodium	1874.2mg
Carbohydrates	58.3g
Protein	40.6g

* Percent Daily Values are based on a 2,000 calorie diet.

CREOLE ANY-NOODLES SALAD

Ingredients

- 4 oz. chopped black olives
- 1 cans sliced mushrooms
- 1/2 red onion, sliced very thin
- 3 small tomatoes, chopped
- 1 small bell pepper, sliced
- 15 oz. artichoke hearts
- 2 sliced cucumbers
- 3 stalks celery
- 8 oz. Italian dressing
- Salad Supreme dry seasoning
- 8 oz. cooked noodles, any
- salt and pepper

Directions

- Prepare the pasta by following the directions on the package. Drain it.
- Get a large mixing bowl: Toss the pasta with the remaining ingredients. Serve it right way.
- Enjoy.

Servings per Recipe: 10

Timing Information:

Preparation	20 mins
Total Time	40 mins

Nutritional Information:

Calories	212.2
Fat	8.9g
Cholesterol	19.1mg
Sodium	633.2mg
Carbohydrates	29.3g
Protein	6.4g

* Percent Daily Values are based on a 2,000 calorie diet.

WHITE FISH AND CREOLE POTATO CASSEROLE

Ingredients

- 2 medium sweet potatoes, sliced
- 1/2 onion, peeled and sliced thinly
- 1/2-3/4 lb white fish fillet
- 1 dash creole seasoning
- 3-5 garlic cloves, peeled
- 4 C. spinach, chopped
- 8 small roma tomatoes, diced

Directions

- Before you do anything, preheat the oven to 450 F.
- Grease a Dutch oven with some olive oil. Lay in it onion slices followed by the white fish fillets. Season them with the Cajun seasoning.
- Top it with potatoes, garlic, onions, and tomatoes. Lay the spinach on top then season them with some salt and pepper.
- Place the pot in the oven and let them cook for 44 min. Serve your fish casserole warm.
- Enjoy.

Servings per Recipe: 4

Timing Information:

Preparation	15 mins
Total Time	1 hr

Nutritional Information:

Calories	143.1
Fat	1.1g
Cholesterol	38.0mg
Sodium	106.7mg
Carbohydrates	20.6g
Protein	13.5g

* Percent Daily Values are based on a 2,000 calorie diet.

OKRA JUMBO STEW

Ingredients

- 2 tbsp vegetable oil
- 1 lb andouille sausage, sliced
- 2 lbs chicken tenders, diced
- 1 medium yellow onion, sliced
- 3 large garlic cloves, chopped
- 3 celery ribs, chopped
- 1 green pepper, thin strips
- 1 red bell pepper, thin strips
- 4 sprigs fresh thyme
- 2 C. chicken stock
- 1 C. tomato juice
- 1/4 C. hot sauce
- 1 lb medium raw shrimp, peeled and deveined
- 8 oz. frozen okra, defrosted
- 1/4 C. fresh flat-leaf parsley, chopped
- 4 scallions, green and white parts, thinly sliced

Directions

- Place a large pan over medium heat. Heat the oil in it.
- Cook in it the sausage for 4 min. Push it to one side of the pan. Cook the chicken tenders on the other side with a pinch of salt and pepper for 4 min.
- Add the onion with garlic, celery, bell peppers, thyme, a pinch of salt and pepper. Mix them all well and let them cook for 6 min.
- Stir in the stock, tomato sauce, and hot sauce. Cook them until they start boiling.
- Stir in the shrimp and okra. Put on the lid and let them cook for 6 min. Fold the parsley and scallions into the stew then serve it hot.
- Enjoy.

Servings per Recipe: 4

Timing Information:

Preparation	0 mins
Total Time	30 mins

Nutritional Information:

Calories	932.2
Fat	44.5g
Cholesterol	372.4mg
Sodium	2426.1mg
Carbohydrates	25.7g
Protein	103.2g

* Percent Daily Values are based on a 2,000 calorie diet.

SMOKED VENISON JERKY

Ingredients

- 2 lbs ground venison
- 1/4 C. Cajun seasoning
- 1/4 C. Worcestershire sauce
- 1/4 C. liquid smoke
- 1 tbsp black pepper

Directions

- Get a large mixing bowl: Stir in it all the ingredients. Spread the mix on the dehydrating trays.
- Dehydrate the jerky for 6 h 20 min on 156 degrees. Serve your jerky right away or store them sealing bags.
- Enjoy.

Servings per Recipe: 15

Timing Information:

Preparation	15 mins
Total Time	24 hrs 15 mins

Nutritional Information:

Calories	99.2
Fat	4.3g
Cholesterol	48.4mg
Sodium	90.5mg
Carbohydrates	1.1g
Protein	13.2g

* Percent Daily Values are based on a 2,000 calorie diet.

MIRACLE TUNA DIP

Ingredients

- 1/3 C. cream cheese, softened
- 3 tbsp Miracle Whip
- 1 tsp paprika
- 1/4 tsp black pepper
- 1/4 tsp garlic powder
- 1/4 tsp ground red pepper
- 1 (6 1/2 oz.) cans tuna, drained and broken into chunks
- 1/4 C. finely chopped bell pepper
- 2 tbsp thinly sliced sweet onions

Directions

- Get a small mixing bowl: Mix in it the cream cheese, Miracle Whip, paprika, black pepper, garlic powder, and red pepper until they become light and smooth.
- Fold the tuna, bell pepper, and onion into the mix. Place the dip in the fridge and let it sit for at least 4 h in the fridge.
- Serve your dip whenever you desire.
- Enjoy.

Servings per Recipe: 9

Timing Information:

Preparation	5 mins
Total Time	5 mins

Nutritional Information:

Calories	62.4
Fat	4.0g
Cholesterol	17.2mg
Sodium	33.7mg
Carbohydrates	0.9g
Protein	5.5g

* Percent Daily Values are based on a 2,000 calorie diet.

Printed in Great Britain
by Amazon

33789029R00057